# Genghis
# Khan

*Series Editor C.S. Nicholls*

Highly readable brief lives of those who have played a significant part in history, and whose contributions still influence contemporary culture.

# Genghis Khan

JAMES CHAMBERS

First published in 1999
This edition published in 2009

The History Press
The Mill, Brimscombe Port
Stroud, Gloucestershire, GL5 2QG
www.thehistorypress.co.uk

British Library Cataloguing in Publication Data.
A catalogue record for this book is available from the British Library.

ISBN 978 0 7524 5474 0

Typesetting and origination by The History Press
Printed in Great Britain

# C O N T E N T S

# A NOTE ON TRANSLITERATION

The vast Mongol Empire, which encompassed many different nations and cultures, presents historians with two so-far insuperable difficulties. First of all, the earliest records were written in such a broad diversity of languages that nobody has yet been able to read all of them in the original. Second, as Dr David Morgan wrote in the introduction to by far the best general work on the subject, 'there is no satisfactory solution to the problem of transliteration when one is dealing with words from so many languages and scripts'.[1]

The consequence of the first difficulty is that some books on the Mongols are inevitably biased towards the author's speciality; and the consequence of the second is that they all contain a variety of justifiable spellings for the names of the same people and places. With some languages the differences are due simply to the development of new systems. Today, for example, most books use *Beijing* to represent the Chinese name for the city that other books called *Peking*. But at the other end of the scale there has never been a universally accepted system of transliteration into English from Mongolian. Even the specialists still differ in their spelling of Mongol names.

The best anyone can do is aim at consistency, and even then there are likely to be compromises. Although the founder of the Mongol Empire is most accurately represented as *Chingiz Khān*, I have used *Genghis Khan* because this is the spelling by which he is best known to English speakers. Similarly, like many recent authors, I have used *Kh* or *K* rather than *Q* throughout, partly because it represents famous names in the form by which they are best known. For example, Genghis Khan's most famous grandson is better known as *Khubilai* rather than *Qubilai*, just as the holy book of Islam is still better known as the *Koran* rather than the *Qur'ān*. For the sake of simplicity, I have also omitted the symbols for umlauts and accents.

Despite the difficulties, however, the variations in books which do not use the same spellings as I have used are very seldom so great as to prevent readers from recognizing the names instantly when, as I hope they will, they go on to read more about the astonishing medieval empire of the Mongol horsemen.

James Chambers

London, 1999

# ACKNOWLEDGEMENTS

I would like to thank Christine Nicholls, Jaqueline Mitchell and Helen Gray for their help and patience in the preparation of this text.

# CHRONOLOGY

# Chronology

# THE SONS OF THE GREY WOLF

Across the heart of the northern hemisphere, from Hungary to China, there are almost a hundred thousand square miles of desolate, treeless grassland known as the steppes. Throughout their long winter most of their earth is frozen solid. In the spring and the autumn their air is often thick with torrential rain. At the height of their short summer the yellow grass is baked brittle. For the most part they are good for very little other than hunting and herding hardy livestock; and they are so inhospitable that many of the people who first lived there moved on as soon as they could, migrating to conquer and settle in the richer soil of Europe, the Middle East or China.

At the eastern end of the steppes, however, the landscape is different. At first the grassland degenerates into a barren desert, the Gobi, but in the north, beyond the desert, there are rich rolling pastures rising amid many rivers to the forested foothills of Mount Kentey, a sacred mountain which was known long ago as Burkhan-Khaldun, 'God's Hill'. The people who live there today are the people who have always lived there and, like the haunted land itself, they are different.

According to their ancient legends, the nomads of the eastern steppes are unlike any other people on earth. At the dawn of time, they say, after the God of Eternal Heaven, Mongke Tengri, had made all the animals, he made the first human beings, moulding them out of clay. But the eastern nomads were not created until later, when the grey wolf, the great hunter, wandered down out of the forests on the side of the sacred mountain. Some say that he mated with a woman. Others say that he mated with a swift tawny doe. But all are agreed that the offspring of this union are the Mongols.

After ten generations, when the Mongols had multiplied, a direct descendant of the grey wolf's firstborn, Dobun the Sagacious married a woman called Alan the Fair, who came from a tribe of hunters in the forest. A few years later, Dobun died suddenly, leaving two infant sons. During the next three years, however, Alan, who did not remarry, gave birth to three more sons. Throughout their childhood and youth, her two elder sons believed understandably that their half-brothers were the children of a handsome young servant whom their father had bought as a boy for a hunk of venison. But when all her sons were grown to manhood, Alan called them together and, as sometimes happens in legends, convinced them that the three younger sons were divine. At the conception of each, she claimed, the God of Eternal Heaven, in the form of a shining golden man, had come down through the smoke-hole in the top of her tent, impregnated her with a ray of light and then, after turning into a yellow dog, returned to heaven on a moonbeam. Later, he had visited her again in a dream and told her that the descendants of her sons would rule the world.

After making her revelation, Alan gave each of her sons an arrow and asked him to break it. When they had all done so, she handed each a bundle of arrows and asked him to break that. When all had failed, she explained her parable. If each stood alone, he would easily be broken, like a single arrow; but if they all stayed loyally together, no power on earth would be strong enough to destroy them.

While Alan lived, her five sons followed her advice. As soon as she was dead, however, the four eldest divided her herds between them, leaving the youngest, Bodunchar the Simple, to ride off alone on the ugly pony that was now all he possessed. When at last his repentant eldest brother came in search of him, Bodunchar was living in a hut on the banks of the river Onon and surviving by hunting duck with a trained hawk and begging mare's milk from a clan that was camped nearby. Back among his brothers, Bodunchar described the people who had befriended him. They had no leader. All their decisions were made in council. If they could be taken by surprise, they could be overwhelmed before they had time to organize their defence. With Bodunchar at their head, the brothers and their followers returned to the easy ambush of his unsuspecting friends and enriched themselves by seizing their herds and enslaving their families.

By the standards of the steppes there was nothing wrong in what Bodunchar and his brothers had done. In truth, as well as in legend, it was the way in which the Turko-Mongol nomads had always lived, and the way in which they were to continue to live for several more generations. These nomads measured each other's wealth by the numbers of their sheep and horses, and when the size of a clan's herds increased, it was usually as a result of audacious raiding rather than patient husbandry. Ruthless opportunists like Bodunchar were regarded as heroes, and their success bred success. Warriors often moved from clan to clan, swearing new allegiances to the men most likely to protect their families and make them rich. Although the tribes and the clans into which they were divided must have begun as extended families, their blood lines were soon diluted, not only because those with the best leaders attracted warriors from elsewhere, but also because it was the custom to marry outside the clan. Since bride prices were high, women were often acquired like horses on raiding parties.

In such a society, life was simple, selfish and precarious. But it was not always to be like this. According to an ancient prophecy, often quoted by the holy men, the shamans, the Mongols would one day be united by a pauper descendant of Bodunchar, who would come to them dressed in a goatskin cloak and mounted on a barren mare. Under his leadership they would become invincible, like Alan's bundle of arrows, and behind his standard they would ride beyond the steppes to win unimaginable riches.

This is the story of the man who fulfilled that prophecy. It is the story of an illiterate nomad called Temuchin, who rose to rule the largest empire ever conquered by a single commander – larger even than the empire of Alexander. It is the story of a military genius who created an army and an administration so effective and efficient that his dominions kept growing after his death until they had become the largest continuous empire the world has ever known. Several hundred years later, the people on the faraway island of Britain were to create an empire that was even larger. But the British Empire was scattered across the globe. The Mongol Empire, stretching eastward from the borders of Hungary to the shores of the China Sea, was all contained within one boundary.

Around the middle of the twelfth century, when legend began to mingle with history, most of the

Mongol tribes were united for the first time under their first khan, Kabul. But their new strength created anxiety at the court of the Chin emperor in Zhongdu, near modern Beijing.

China was no longer a united empire. Only the south was now ruled by a true Chinese dynasty, the Sung. At the beginning of the tenth century the north, including the great city of Zhongdu, had been invaded and conquered by Khitan horsemen from the steppes. At the end of that century the weakened Sung empire had been reduced still further when the Tangut inhabitants of north-western China had seceded and established their own kingdom of Hsi-Hsia. Then, early in the following century, the north had been wrested from the Khitan conquerors by another wave of horsemen, this time Jurchen from Manchuria. A few of the Khitan fled north-east beyond Korea and the remnants of their last army followed one of their princes westward to the distant steppes beyond the Hindu Kush, where they eventually built the Buddhist empire of Kara-Khitai, 'Black Cathay'. But the majority of those who had not fallen in battle remained in China to become subjects of the Jurchen, who took over Zhongdu and installed a savage and ostentatious new dynasty, which they called Chin, 'Golden'.

The Chin knew only too well that what their ancestors had done could be done again by others. As they feared, contingents from the Mongol confederacy were soon making raids across their borders. In order to pre-empt any full-scale invasion therefore, they sent ambassadors to the Tatars, one of the most powerful and belligerent tribes outside the confederacy, and bribed them to attack it with promises of supplies and rewards. With Chin support, the Tatars had little difficulty in breaking up the confederacy. But their armies were not always successful in open battle. There were a few Mongol commanders who were able to outmanoeuvre them, and one of these was Yesugei, leader of the small Kiyat clan, who claimed descent from Bodunchar.

Yesugei attracted warriors from many other clans to his banner, and he made a formidable alliance with Toghril, king of the mysterious Christian Keraits. While most of the peoples on the eastern steppes still believed in a huge hierarchy of gods and spirits, with whom the shamans acted as intermediaries on their behalf, the Kereits had been converted to a form of Christianity by Persian followers of Nestorius, the fifth-century patriarch of Constantinople who was deposed for denying that the Virgin Mary could be regarded as the Mother of God. Their faith did little to modify their conduct, however. Toghril won his throne at the end of an ugly, fratricidal civil war, in which the arrival of Yesugei and his band of experienced professionals finally tipped the balance in his favour. The two men became blood brothers, *anda*, and in gratitude for his support Toghril swore a solemn oath of eternal friendship to Yesugei, his children and his children's children.

Like many Mongols, Yesugei stole his first wife, although in this case the incident engendered uncustomary resentment because the lady was already another man's bride. She was Ho'elun of the Onggirats, a tribe whose women were famous for their beauty. Her husband was a prince in one of the largest tribes, the Merkits, and he was bringing her home when they were ambushed by Yesugei and his two brothers. Knowing that her new husband was no match for three men,

Ho'elun persuaded him to run for his life and, after pulling off her smock and throwing it to him as a keepsake, waited quietly for her inevitable fate. Yesugei had chosen even better than he realized: the beautiful Ho'elun transferred her loyalty to him and his clan for ever, and in time her courage, common sense and energy were to be all that stood between his family and oblivion.

Ho'elun bore Yesugei four sons, Temuchin, Kasar, Kachun and Temuge, and one daughter, Temulun; and by his second wife, Suchigu, Yesugei had two more sons, Bekhter and Belgutei. Some say that the eldest, Temuchin, which means man of iron, or blacksmith, was named after a Tatar commander whom Yesugei had captured shortly before his birth, but it seems more likely that iron was simply a favourite theme of Yesugei's since he used it again for another son, Temuge, and a daughter, Temulun.

Mongols cared little for age. Few of them knew how old they were. As a result, the date of Temuchin's birth was unrecorded and remains uncertain. However, since it was said that he was born in a 'year of the pig', the most probable year was 1167. Like all Mongol boys, Temuchin learned to ride and shoot a bow when he was very young. In his lessons and his games, his companions were his brother Kasar, his half-brothers Bekhter and Belgutei, who were older than his other full brothers, and above all a friend from another camp, Jamuka, heir to the leadership of Jadirat clan. Along the banks of the River Onon, Temuchin and Jamuka conducted imaginary hunts and led imaginary armies, and one day, in an earnest ceremony, they exchanged gifts and swore the eternal vows of blood brothers.

When Temuchin was only nine years old, Yesugei decided to strengthen the uneasy alliance which his marriage to Ho'elun had imposed on her people by arranging a more willing marriage between their eldest son and the daughter of one of the Onggirat chiefs. With Temuchin at his side, he set out for the Onggirat pastures, which lay far off near the northern end of the Great Wall of China. Before they found the camp of Ho'elun's clan, however, they rested for the night at another Onggirat camp, where the chief was greatly impressed by Temuchin. The boy was tall for his age and already had the piercing 'cat's eyes' and quiet dignity that were to inspire so many men in the future. Protesting that his own women were as beautiful as any Onggirats, the chief offered one of his daughters, Bortei, as a bride. Yesugei was equally impressed and accepted. The terms of the marriage were agreed. In accordance with the tradition among chiefs, Temuchin was left to live with Bortei's family for a while, to learn their ways and to share some of his childhood with his future bride. As he mounted to ride away, Yesugei anxiously warned his new friend that his son was afraid of dogs.

On the journey home Yesugei halted to share a meal with a small group of herdsmen. It was customary to offer hospitality to travellers on the steppes, but these men were Tatars and one of them recognized the unsuspecting Yesugei as a commander who had once defeated and plundered them. As he continued his journey, growing weaker and weaker, Yesugei realized that they had put slow poison in his food. Back at his camp, he summoned his friend and servant Monglik to his bedside, ordered him to bring Temuchin home from the Onggirats and warned him to say only that he was missing his son and not to reveal that he was dying. Monglik, as always, obeyed the order, but by the time Temuchin returned, his father was dead.

The strong, skilful leader had been succeeded by a helpless nine-year-old boy. The warriors who had sworn allegiance to Yesugei returned to their former clans, taking with them their families, their sheep and their horses, and the Tayichi'uts, close kinsmen of the Kiyats, who made up the majority of these warriors, gratuitously humiliated his widow by excluding her from their religious ceremonies.

Ho'elun and her family withdrew to the upper reaches of the River Onon, between the steppes and the forest, in the foothills of the sacred mountain. Here they kept themselves alive for several years by hunting and fishing and picking wild berries. They were unmolested simply because they were too poor to be worth the risk of providing one of Yesugei's former allies with an excuse for vengeful retaliation.

The surviving records of Temuchin's early life were not written until long after he had become master of an empire. It may be therefore that they exaggerated the poverty of his childhood to make a dramatic contrast with his later achievements,

just as those that were written by his descendants'
courtiers sometimes omitted episodes which might
reflect badly on the reputation of the great ancestor.
Nevertheless, even the source closest to the steppes,
*The Secret History of the Mongols*, described the
deprivations suffered by Ho'elun and her family,
and this is the only source which also recounted
the more shameful episodes in the life of the future
khan.

One such episode was the death of Temuchin's
half-brother Bekhter. There seems to have been
a rivalry for leadership of the family between
the eldest sons of Yesugei's two widows. When
Temuchin was about thirteen the rivalry came
to a head in a quarrel over game. Ignoring the
custom of the steppes, Bekhter and his brother
Belgutei refused to share their kills with their
brothers and sometimes stole the game that the
others had killed. Although Ho'elun advised her
sons to ignore it, Temuchin and Kasar decided
to take action. They crept up on Bekhter while
he was taking his turn at guarding their precious
horses while they grazed, and drew their bows. He
heard them and turned. When it became clear that
pleading for his life was futile, he pleaded only that

his innocent brother Belgutei should be spared. Temuchin and Kasar agreed and then loosed their arrows.

When she deduced what had happened from their sullen silence, Ho'elun was outraged. According to *The Secret History of the Mongols*, which was almost certainly written by someone close to Temuchin, she berated her murderous sons for quarrelling among themselves when they had no companions but their shadows and were not even strong enough to avenge the betrayal and insults done to them by the Tayichi'uts. As for Belgutei, despite his brother's murder, he stayed with his father's family and grew up to be one of Temuchin's closest and most valued counsellors.

Soon afterwards the Tayichi'uts attacked Ho'elun's little camp. At the first sight of them the family fled into the forest. While the women and two youngest boys hid in a ditch, Belgutei built a barricade with logs and Temuchin and Kasar, who was already earning a reputation as an archer, held off their assailants with their bows. But the leader of the Tayichi'uts called out that the only one they wanted was Temuchin.

When she heard this, Ho'elun put her son on a horse and told him to run. The Tayichi'uts set out after him and eventually surrounded him in a thicket. After nine long days, when their starving quarry tried to slip past them by moonlight, they captured him.

None of the surviving accounts give any reason for this attack. Temuchin's commanding presence was already being talked about across the steppes, and it may be therefore that the Tayichi'uts were afraid that he might one day attract his own band of warriors and punish them for deserting his mother, or it may be that they had heard about the murder of Bekhter and had taken it upon themselves to avenge it, particularly since they treated him like a criminal. He was locked into a *cangue*, a heavy wooden collar like a yoke with long wings resting on the shoulders, to which the prisoner's wrists were tied. By day he was displayed in a cage in the centre of the camp, and by night each family was required to take its turn guarding him in its tent.

One evening, after many weeks, when the Tayichi'uts were preoccupied with the carousing that followed the Festival of the Red Moon,

Temuchin stunned his guard with the end of the *cangue*, crept out of the camp and hid in the reeds beside the bank of the river. When the guard regained consciousness he raised the alarm. In the drunken, disorganized search that followed, Temuchin was discovered, not by one of the Tayichi'uts but by Sorkan, a member of the small Suldu clan, which had come as it did every year to pay tribute to them. Sorkan had no quarrel with Temuchin. He persuaded the others in his party that the prisoner was not in the reeds. When they had all moved on, Temuchin worked his way downriver to the Suldu camp, where Sorkan's family took off his *cangue* and burned it and then hid him in a cartload of wool. On the following evening, when the search had been called off, Sorkan gave Temuchin some food, a cloak and his least valuable horse and sent him off into the darkness.

Several days later, at their new campsite beside the River Onon, Ho'elun and her family looked up and saw a tall horseman cantering towards them out of the steppes. It was Temuchin, dressed in a goatskin cloak and mounted on a barren mare.

# THE PAUPER
# PRINCE

Temuchin returned from his escape to a family that was as destitute as it had been before his capture. They still lived by hunting and gathering berries, only now they also covered their tracks, and the felt tent which sheltered all of them was moved regularly in the hope of avoiding a return visit from the Tayichi'uts. Their only valuable possessions were nine geldings, and it was not long before most of these were lost.

One day, when Belgutei had taken one of the precious horses to hunt marmots on the steppes, a large group of warriors swooped on the little camp, cut the tethers on the eight others and drove them away. With no other mounts on which to give chase, Temuchin and his brothers watched helplessly as the raiders and their horses disappeared over the horizon.

When Belgutei returned, Temuchin took his horse and set out after them. Three days later, in the dim light of early morning, he came across a young man milking a small herd of mares. It was thirteen-year-old Bo'orchu, son of Nayan the Rich, whose tribe had once been allies of Yesugei. Bo'orchu had never met Temuchin before, but when he heard what had happened he gave him a fresh mare, took another for himself and set out with him to find his geldings.

After another three days, at dusk, they saw the thieves' camp in the distance. Temuchin recognized his horses in their makeshift corral. When night fell, the two young men crept in, cut out the eight geldings and made off with them in the darkness. As they rode home, Temuchin offered to give Bo'orchu some of the horses as a reward, but Bo'orchu refused to accept them, and the two parted with vows of undying friendship.

Not long afterwards, when he was almost sixteen, Temuchin set out with Belgutei to find the camp where his father had betrothed him to Bortei. As the head of a family with one tent and nine horses, he was hardly a worthy match for the daughter of an Onggirat chief. But the young descendant of Bodunchar was still made welcome. Bortei's father consented to the marriage, and when Temuchin and his bride returned to his camp her mother went with them and presented Ho'elun with a magnificent black sable cloak.

Sable was the most precious commodity on the steppes. The cloak was a gift fit for a king, and Temuchin and his mother made good use of it. Temuchin sent Belgutei to summon Bo'orchu, and then, with these two and Kasar as his escorts, he rode to the camp of the Christian Keraits, knelt before the throne of Toghril, their king, and presented him with the black sable cloak.

'In times gone by you swore the vows of *anda* with my father,' he said. 'Therefore you are as a father to me. I have brought home a bride, and I now bring to you, as to my father, my bride's gift for her new parents.'

Toghril accepted the gift and, renewing the vows he had made with his father, recognized Temuchin as a son. 'In return for the black sable cloak,' he said, 'I will unite you with your scattered people.'[1]

Temuchin was now the poorest of Toghril's many vassals. But, unlike the others, who were regarded as inferior brothers, Temuchin was an adopted son. From then on he made regular visits to the Kerait camp. He became a favourite courtier. He learned the ways of a nomad king. His reputation grew. An old blacksmith, a swordmaker, remembered a promise he had made to Yesugei and came down from his forge on the sacred mountain to present Temuchin with his son Jelme as a servant.

With the addition of Bo'orchu and now Jelme, Temuchin had the beginnings of his own clan. But he was still a long way from being able to survive without his powerful protector, and he had found him only just in time.

Like his reputation, the news of his marriage spread across the steppes and reached the encampments of the Merkits. The Merkits had a longstanding score to settle. When Yesugei stole a Merkit's bride, he had been too powerful to challenge. But now there was a new bride in the family, and the family was no longer strong. The time had come for retribution.

Three hundred Merkits found Temuchin's camp and charged it as the sun rose. Temuchin and his family heard them before they saw them, and when they saw them it was obvious that resistance would be futile. The men would be killed and the women would be captured anyway. They leapt on their horses and galloped for the cover of the forests in the foothills of the holy mountain, from which they never dared to move far. But there were not enough horses. There was a horse for each of the men. There was a horse for Ho'elun, who took her daughter Temulun on the saddle in front of her to save her from a Merkit's bed. There was even a packhorse. But there was no horse for Suchigu and no horse for Bortei. The junior widow and the new bride were left to their inevitable fate. By the standards of the steppes the survival of the men was more important and, since the women would not be killed, there was always a chance that they could be recovered on another raid.

Suchigu and Bortei were captured and led away. Back at the Merkit camp, Bortei was forced to sleep with the younger brother of the prince from whom her husband's father had stolen Ho'elun. Meanwhile, Temuchin turned for help to Toghril. The Kerait king had no love for the Merkits. He had been their prisoner as a child. In response to Temuchin's appeal, he put twenty thousand men in the field and sent messengers to summon support from one of his other vassals, Temuchin's childhood friend Jamuka, who was now leader of the Jadarat.

Like Temuchin, Jamuka had spent part of his youth in peril; and like Toghril, he had a score to settle with the Merkits. Although his warriors had not abandoned him when he succeeded his neglectful father, they had been scattered soon afterwards when the Merkits overwhelmed them and plundered their camp. For a while Jamuka had wandered the steppes with only thirty followers, until in desperation he had been forced to swear allegiance to the Merkits and enter their service. In the end he had managed to recover his herds, and with them his tribe, only by tricking his way into the Merkit chief's tent and holding him to ransom. Calling support from some of his allies, Jamuka rode to the rendezvous with another twenty thousand men.

The combined Kerait and Jadarat army routed the Merkits in a surprise night attack. While Toghril and Jamuka plundered their camp, Temuchin was reunited with Bortei. But Belgutei was not reunited with his mother, Suchigu. She was so ashamed of being forced to sleep with a Merkit that, when her son entered the tent where she had been held, she ran out, calling through her tears that she was no longer fit to stand before him, and disappeared forever into the forest.

Soon after Bortei was restored to her husband, almost nine months after her capture, she gave birth to her first son, Jochi. Inevitably there was doubt about the boy's legitimacy, but if Temuchin shared it he never showed it. Throughout his life he was always careful to show equal affection to all the children that Bortei bore. As time passed he was to have many wives and they were to bear him many sons, but only Bortei sat beside him as empress and only her sons inherited his empire.

After the raid on the Merkits, Jamuka and Temuchin established a joint camp beside the River Onon, where the first of a small but steady stream of adventurers came to swear allegiance to the pauper chieftain who had been adopted by the king of the Keraits. The two old friends renewed the vows of *anda* which they had first sworn as children, and for the next eighteen months they were inseparable. But in reality they were rivals. If the Mongols were ever again to be united under one khan, as many of them still hoped, Jamuka and Temuchin were both leading candidates for the role. Eventually, on Bortei's advice, Temuchin withdrew to a camp of his own.

At the new camp the flow of recruits increased. They were drawn to Temuchin not only by his powerful new connection but also by his reputation for sharing everything with his followers, by the uncanny magnetism that had already made men like Sorkan and Bo'orchu risk their lives for him, and by his equally alluring sense of destiny. Temuchin believed that he had only survived so many misfortunes because heaven had singled him out for greatness. The influential shamans supported his belief, and the most famous of them, the unscrupulous Kokochu, who was the son of Yesugei's old servant Monglik, convinced thousands that he had ascended into heaven in a trance and had been told by Mongke Tengri, the supreme god himself, that the whole world would be given to Temuchin and his sons.

At the same time Jamuka's camp was also growing. There were now many men in it besides his own Jadirat. But for the most part they were obedient clansmen who had followed their chiefs to the standard of a successful leader. The men who came to Temuchin were men who had chosen him for themselves. They came from many different tribes, not in clans but in small groups or even alone, and among them came Jelme's cunning brother Subodei, who was soon to be Temuchin's most successful general and who was destined to rank beside him in the pages of history as one of the greatest commanders of all time.

Apart from Temuchin and Jamuka, there were several other possible candidates for the role of Mongol khan. But in the surviving assessment of an old Tayichi'ut chief, who had no reason to be biased in his favour, only Temuchin had the style and judgement of a leader. His new tribe and his family agreed. In the summer of 1185, when Temuchin was only eighteen years old, his cousins, who had until then ignored him, brought their clans to his camp and together with his own followers elected him as their khan.

It was a long way from being khan of all the Mongols. Temuchin's rule extended only to the clans of his own tribe, the Borjigid, and the electors intended that his authority should be limited to absolute leadership in time of war.

In the days that followed the election, however, any kinsmen who had hoped to retain a degree of independence must have looked on anxiously as the new khan gave them a first taste of things to come. Temuchin organized his camp in a way that no Mongol camp had been organized before. For training and combat, he divided all the warriors into two groups, light mounted archers and heavy cavalry, and he created his own elite unit with similar divisions, 'Quiver Bearers' and 'Sword Bearers'. For the everyday management of the camp, he divided everyone again into smaller groups with specific responsibilities – taking care of the horses or the sheep, guarding and distributing the supplies of food and water, maintaining the wagons – and the overall authority for all administration was given to Temuchin's two first followers, Jelme and Bo'orchu.

Toghril was delighted at the news of his adopted son's election, but Jamuka recognized it as a threat. The vows of *anda* were forgotten. He sent messengers to other chiefs, urging them to join him in destroying the ambitious upstart before it was too late, and then, in 1187, when he had assembled thirty thousand horsemen drawn from fourteen different tribes, he declared war, ostensibly in retribution because one of Temuchin's followers had killed a Jadirat for nothing more than stealing a few horses.

By then Temuchin had amassed almost as many men. But neither he nor they were ready for action. In the first great battle of his life, fought at Dalan Balzhut, 'The Seventy Marshes', Temuchin was defeated. Yet, despite the setback, his followers stayed with him as he withdrew towards the cover of the northern snows, and within days Jamuka's conduct had served to increase their numbers. Instead of pursuing his defeated enemy, Jamuka attacked some of the clans that had not supported him and executed seventy of his leading prisoners by boiling them in cauldrons.

The Mongols were not cruel. They were pitiless. They believed that the spirits of men ranked below those of animals in the great cosmic hierarchy. A man's short time on earth was worth very little to them. Since there was no other practical way of dealing with prisoners who could not be trusted, they were often slaughtered in large numbers. But they were killed quickly. Torture was rare among the Mongols, and it was usually only inflicted on those who had perpetrated some atrocity themselves. Revolted by Jamuka's brutality, two whole tribes and many other warriors abandoned him and set out towards the bleak north in search of Temuchin.

# THE WAR OF THE BROTHERS

The nine years which followed the defeat at Dalan Balzhut are a mystery. Nobody knows for certain where Temuchin went or what he did. Some said that he and his men entered the service of the Chin emperor, and it is true that when they next appeared in reliable records they were fighting for the Chin against the Tatars. In their successful campaign to destroy the Mongol confederacy, the Chin had turned the Tatars into the most powerful force in the eastern steppes, and as a result one of history's regular patterns had repeated itself. The mercenary allies had replaced the defeated enemy as the most serious threat to their employer's security.

With the Mongols divided, there was little left for the Tatars to do other than assist the Chin in campaigns against troublesome border tribes.

By 1190 some of them had begun to conduct raids of their own into Chin territory. In 1195, during a joint campaign against the Onggirat, the Tatar leader quarrelled with the Chin general over the distribution of spoils and withdrew his support, leaving the Chin army so weakened that the Onggirat were able to make a successful counter-attack. In the following spring, however, Temuchin cornered the rebel Tatars in a forest to the north of the Gobi. Their leader was among the many who died when the Mongols broke through their spiked barricades, and all his treasure was carried away, including his splendid gold bed encrusted with pearls.

Soon after this engagement, Toghril and the remnants of his royal retinue emerged from the desert in search of Temuchin. The Keraits had again been divided by civil war. Toghril had been deposed by his brother, who had been supported by the Naimans, a huge Turkish tribe which roamed the flat steppes to the west of them. Temuchin returned to Mongolia and, like his father before him, restored the old Kerait king to his throne, only this time it was achieved without a battle. At the approach of Temuchin's well-trained, disciplined and possibly experienced army, the Naimans and their puppet vanished.

In gratitude for Temuchin's victory over the Tatars, the Chin had appointed him a Deputy Commissioner for the Border. Now, in the hope of winning a new ally and restoring the balance of power on the steppes, they gave Toghril the title of a Chinese prince, Wang. Forever afterwards the king of the Keraits was known as Wang Khan; and it was this title, pronounced 'Ong' by the Mongols, which a century later led the Venetian traveller Marco Polo to identify him as Prester John, the legendary Christian king of the Orient.

In 1199, when they had re-established themselves on the steppes, Wang Khan and Temuchin rode west to punish and neutralize the Naimans. After chasing one Naiman army into the Altai Mountains, they were returning to the steppes when they met another blocking their path. Since night was falling, the two armies camped in battle order and waited for dawn. But when the sun rose there was nothing left of the Keraits but their smouldering camp fires. Wang Khan had crept away in the darkness.

Temuchin withdrew cautiously and headed home on a loop round the eastern end of the mountains. Prudently, the Naiman commander ignored him and set out after the Keraits instead. A few days later a desperate Kerait messenger galloped into Temuchin's camp. Wang Khan had been ambushed. The Naimans had captured half his army and made off with almost all his herds. At once Temuchin dispatched a division, and, at its first charge, the Naimans broke off an attack on the remains of the Kerait army and abandoned their plunder and their prisoners.

In his old age, the once unscrupulous king of the Keraits was becoming timid and indecisive, and his brother's recent coup had left him paranoid. He had deserted his ally because Jamuka had fed him false reports that Temuchin was negotiating secretly with the Naimans and had convinced him that, like his brother, his Mongol 'son' was planning to seize his throne. Now that the magnanimous rescue had proved him wrong, Wang Khan was sentimentally penitent and grateful. He renewed the vows of *anda* with his adopted son, and he showered gifts on Bo'orchu, who had led the Mongol charge.

For Wang Khan's only son by blood, Prince Senggum, the rescue and the reconciliation were far from reassuring. Although it was not in Temuchin's nature to intrigue against an ally, it was obvious that he did indeed aspire to be Wang Khan's heir; and in his praise for Temuchin and his open contempt for Senggum, the old man had led each of them to hope or fear that it might happen. The rescue had been more cynically self-interested than magnanimous. If Temuchin hoped to be Wang Khan's heir, he had no choice but to stay in favour with him; and there was no point in being heir if there was going to be nothing left to inherit.

Having failed to divide the alliance, Jamuka decided to challenge it instead. Manipulating their suspicion of Temuchin's ambition and their resentment at the prospect of being dominated by Keraits, he persuaded the leaders of almost all the unaligned tribes and clans to assemble for a great council, a *khuriltai*. They met in 1200, in the valley of the River Argun, and in scornful defiance of the Kerait king and Temuchin, Khan of the Borjigin, they elected Jamuka Gurkhan overlord of all the khans. War was inevitable. Wang Khan and Temuchin set out to fight for survival with the odds heavily against them. The advancing army of Jamuka's coalition was even larger than their own, and it contained many of Temuchin's old enemies. The Tayichi'uts, who had once held him prisoner, were among them, and so were the survivors from his vengeful attack on the Merkits, who had stolen his bride. There were even a few clans from the Tatars and the Naimans.

At the end of the year the two armies met to decide the future of the eastern steppes at Koyitan on the southern end of the Argun valley. But the gods and the spirits intervened, engulfing the battlefield in such a violent snowstorm that the horsemen could hardly move or see each other. One by one the clans in Jamuka's uneasy alliance withdrew from the field and turned for home. Eventually Jamuka himself pulled out. Before he rode away, however, he gave in to temptation and rewarded his men by plundering the camps of some of his allies. At one stroke the alliance was ended and Jamuka's brief rule as Gurkhan was over.

When the storm cleared, Temuchin seized the opportunity for retribution and set out after the Tayichi'uts. After a brief but bloody battle, the Tayichi'ut warriors broke up and fled in all directions, abandoning their camp. As always the camp was plundered and the women and children were taken away as slaves, and in addition, on Temuchin's orders, the prisoners from the battle and all the men in the camp were executed. As he rode through the camp surrounded by slaughter, Temuchin heard a woman calling his name. She was Kada'an, the daughter of Sorkan, the man who had helped him to escape from the Tayichi'ut camp. When he recognized her, Temuchin leapt from his horse and they fell into each other's arms. Kada'an was distraught: she was married to a Tayichi'ut and her husband was among the prisoners. Temuchin immediately sent a man to find him, but it was too late. He was already dead. The only consolation that Temuchin could offer was to honour Kada'an by having her seated beside him that evening when his army feasted. Next day, her father and her brothers rode into the camp and were welcomed by a grateful Temuchin into the ranks of his army.

The brief campaign against the Tayichi'uts also introduced Temuchin to another of his great generals, Todoge of the Besuts, whose clan, like Sorkan's, were vassals of the Tayichi'uts. He had fought prominently in the battle, and when he was captured a few days later he issued a defiant challenge, offering to fight any man in the Mongol army. Bo'orchu accepted, and Temuchin gave him his own white-nosed stallion for the combat.

The two great soldiers galloped towards each other, weaving like polo players so as not to present steady targets, and guiding their horses with their legs and heels, so that both hands were free for their bows and bowstrings. Bo'orchu shot first and missed. Todoge shot low. Bo'orchu fell as Temuchin's horse stumbled beneath him. In the next instant, while Temuchin's dismayed warriors were distracted by the death throes of his charger, Todoge galloped past them and headed for the safety of the hills. A few days later, when he returned to the camp and offered to serve Temuchin or die, Temuchin appointed him commander of a troop and gave him a new name, Jebe, 'the Arrow'.

The easy massacre of the Tayichi'uts emboldened Temuchin to plan a much more ambitious campaign of retribution, the annihilation of the Tatars. It was a formidable undertaking: only a generation earlier the Tatars alone had been strong enough to take on all the other Mongol tribes. But it was also necessary: there could be no concord on the eastern steppes while the Tatars remained a force to be reckoned with.

Before the campaign began, Temuchin issued new standing orders. He abolished the old custom that Mongols could take plunder in battle whenever and wherever they found it. From now on all plunder belonged to Temuchin. He would be responsible for distributing it, and no man was to pause for plunder until the order had been given. From now on military objectives came first.

In 1202 at the battle of Dalan-nemurges, 'The Seventy Felt Cloaks', which was fought where the River Khalkha enters Lake Buyur, Temuchin's tightly controlled, well-trained and disciplined army defeated the superior massed clans of the Tatars, killing thousands and capturing many thousands more. The days that followed were devoted to systematic extermination. While all the females and the smallest male children were enslaved as usual, every male Tatar who stood taller than the axle of a wagon was put to death.

The destruction of the Tatars clearly demonstrated that Temuchin and his followers were now one of the most powerful forces on the eastern steppes. His rival Jamuka was left with few options. Jamuka's own conduct had precluded any hope of creating another confederacy. The only united nomad nations capable of equalling Temuchin's numbers were the Keraits to the south, who were his allies, and the Naimans to the west, who for the time being preferred to watch and wait.

Jamuka decided to try again with the Keraits. His blood brother Temuchin was also the adopted brother of Senggum, but he was the obstacle to both their ambitions. Jamuka befriended Senggum, sympathized with him and fuelled his malicious envy of Temuchin; and at that very moment Temuchin played into his hands. Confident in his new power and eager to strengthen his chances of becoming Wang Khan's heir, he sent messengers to the old king proposing a marriage between his eldest son Jochi and Senggum's youngest daughter.

Senggum was outraged at the prospect of a Kerait princess marrying a mere Mongol. His disdainful refusal was so offensive that it might well have provoked a military response if it had not been followed soon afterwards by an apparent change of heart. Persuaded by Jamuka that the best way to get rid of Temuchin would be to capture him, Senggum sent a second messenger agreeing to the marriage and inviting Temuchin to a banquet to celebrate the betrothal. The old Kerait king was deeply distressed by the treachery, but he was now feeble-minded and terrified of Senggum's rages. Although he warned the conspirators that the gods would not protect them, he was powerless to stop them.

For a moment Temuchin's judgement was clouded by his aspirations. He accepted the invitation and set out for the banquet with an escort of only ten horsemen. On the way, however, he rested for the night at the camp of his father's old servant, Mongklik. Mongklik could not believe that a prince who had refused a marriage so contemptuously could change his mind so easily. The banquet had to be a trap. Next morning, disillusioned and bitter, Temuchin rode back to his Mongol camp.

As soon as they realized that the plot had failed, Senggum and Jamuka called together their commanders and planned to set out next day on a surprise attack. The combination of Jamuka's clans and the Kerait army gave them numerical superiority; with the added advantage of surprise they had a good chance of victory. That evening, however, when one of the Kerait commanders was discussing the plans with his wife and son, he was overheard by two herdsmen outside his tent. Selecting their strongest horses, the two men rode through the night and next day brought the warning to Temuchin.

There was no time to prepare a defence. Temuchin gave orders to abandon everything that was not essential for survival and set out north-eastwards towards the empty pastures that had once been occupied by the Tatars. His enemies caught up with him and forced him to stand at Kalakalzhit-elet, not far from the site of his victory at Dalan-nemurges. In a series of charges and counter-charges the casualties were heavy on both sides. But in the end Temuchin was only saved from destruction when Senggum was wounded by an arrow in the neck.

The Keraits gathered round their prince and fell back. The lull in their onslaught gave

Temuchin the chance for a counter-attack, but he was too weak to take it. Instead he withdrew from the field, continued his flight into the far north and hid what was left of his army in the swamps of Baljuna.

The allies did not follow. Temuchin was no longer a threat. Between them Senggum and Jamuka could still raise 40,000 men, while the highest estimate of Temuchin's strength was only 4,600. But the best of his men had survived. He still had Jelme and Bo'orchu, the first of the faithful, Subodei the strategist, dashing Jebe and Mukali, the brilliant orphan who had been adopted by his mother Ho'elun. His brothers were with him, and so were his sons, Jochi, Chaghatai, Ogodei and thirteen-year-old Tolui; and soon, as once before, the best of the Mongols were to join him in adversity. His wife's tribe, the Onggirats, came west to support him, and the prospect of a nomad world dominated by Jamuka and Senggum brought many others, including even Keraits, to his standard.

Temuchin recognized how much they were risking for him. If they challenged the Keraits again and lost, they would all be hunted down and killed. In return for their commitment, he swore that when the great task was completed they would all share the fruits of victory; and together they sealed their covenant by drinking a toast drawn from the bitter waters of the swamp. Years later, when they were masters of an empire, the proud men who had been with the khan in that darkest hour were revered as 'the Muddy Water Drinkers'.

The speed and stealth of Mongol horsemen under Temuchin's command were soon to bewilder the best generals in the most advanced civilizations on earth. In 1203 Temuchin and his army came back from the swamp, covering the last part of their journey by night, and launched a meticulously planned surprise attack on the camp where Wang Khan and his Keraits were feasting.

The Keraits' hugely superior numbers were meaningless. They were camped at the end of the narrow Gorge of Jer, where the River Kerulen cuts through the Heights of Checher. Their escape routes at either end were blocked by many ranks of heavy cavalry and mounted archers. There were archers in the hills on either side, and there were mounted archers cantering round and round their circle of wagons. The more they came out from the cover of the wagons, the more they exposed themselves to arrows.

For three days and three nights the Keraits fought valiantly. During the first night they made many attempts to break out, but the only group that escaped to the hills was the royal bodyguard with Wang Khan and Senggum. After that the remainder stayed on the defensive until exhaustion and despair drove them to surrender.

In the distribution of plunder, the most valuable prizes, Wang Khan's golden tent, his gold cups and dishes and all his servants, were given to the two herdsmen who had warned Temuchin of the approaching army. But this time there was no slaughter. Temuchin's ambition was to rule the Keraits not to destroy them. Once he had been enthroned in Wang Khan's place, the Kerait soldiers and their commanders swore a new oath of allegiance and were dispersed among the units of the Mongol army.

At last the families of the royal Keraits and the divine Borjigid were united in compulsory marriages. Temuchin himself married Wang Khan's elder niece, Ibaka, although he passed her on soon afterwards to the chief of another clan; and his youngest son, Tolui, married not only the other niece, Sorkaktani, but also Wang Khan's granddaughter, Dokuz-Khatun. Marriage to a Mongol was a fate that few Kerait princesses would have relished, but through her marriage to Tolui, the scheming Sorkaktani was destined to become one of the most powerful women in Asia. She was to be the mother of the first Il-khan of Persia, Hulegu, and of two supreme khans of the Mongol empire, Mongke and the great Khubilai, founder of the Yuan dynasty in China.

As for the old king and his son, their freedom was short-lived. Senggum fled south to the Gobi Desert, where he became an unsuccessful bandit and was eventually killed for his crimes. Wang Khan fled westward for almost six hundred miles until he reached the grazing grounds of the Naimans, where the captain of a border patrol refused to believe that the bedraggled old man was a king and killed him. When the truth became known, the khan of the Naimans sent for Wang Khan's skull and had it mounted in silver.

The Naiman khan, to whom the Chin emperor had given the title 'Great King', Tayang-khan was now the only ruler on the eastern steppes capable of surpassing Temuchin's numbers on a battlefield. Inevitably Jamuka came to him. Tayang-khan was cautious, but his son Kuchlug and his generals were confident and eager for action, and he allowed himself to be persuaded. In an effort to raise as many men as he could, he sent messengers to the border of China calling for help from the Ongguts, who like himself were Turks and Nestorian Christians. But the Ongguts refused and warned Temuchin.

In the summer of 1204, Temuchin rode west and met the Naimans and Jamuka's Mongols at Chakirma'ut, in the foothills of the Altai range, near Mount Naqu. He was, as expected, heavily outnumbered. But when Jamuka saw Temuchin's forces on the morning of battle, even he knew that Temuchin was going to win. Since his victory over Temuchin at Dalan Balzhut seventeen years earlier, he had not had a proper chance to see his blood brother in action. At Koyitan he had been blinded by snow. At Kalakalzhit-elet Temuchin's men had been fighting a chaotic, desperate rearguard action. What he saw now, however, was very different from the mass of mounted tribesmen that he had seen at Dalan Balzhut. These were soldiers, similarly equipped, drawn up in neat ranks and deployed in troops, squadrons, regiments and brigades. In the centre at the rear stood Temuchin, mounted on a white horse and surrounded by his staff. Here and there dispatch riders cantered backwards and forwards between the command centre and forward units. This was an army.

The drummer on the camel on Temuchin's left pounded his huge kettledrum. On his right the standard, a wooden cross bedecked with nine yak tails, waved a signal. Black and white flags repeated the signal in front of each brigade. In response the army began to manoeuvre with the precision of the Chin emperor's guards on a parade ground. Jamuka remained to watch no longer. By the time the two forces were engaged, he and his followers had left the field.

Temuchin was lavish in his sincere praise for the heroism of the Naimans. They fought magnificently but without method or co-ordinated tactics. At the end of the day, it was said, their bodies lay packed together like felled logs in a forest. Their khan died with them, but the son who had forced him to fight escaped and eventually found refuge in Kara-Khitai.

When news of Temuchin's victory reached them, most of Jamuka's followers deserted him. For a while he hid in the Tannu mountains, until in the spring of 1205 two of his last companions took him prisoner and brought him to Temuchin. They did not know that the crime which Temuchin abhorred above all others was the betrayal of a rightful leader. Jamuka was too dangerous to be left alive, but before he was executed he was allowed to watch while the men who had betrayed him were beheaded.

At the age of thirty-nine, Temuchin was now master of central Asia. In the spring of 1206 representatives from all the Mongol tribes and clans and the other nomad nations that were now his subjects came to a Great Khuriltai beneath the sacred mountain at the source of the River Onon. The great task was completed and the men who had made it possible were rewarded with ranks and riches. Among them, Sorkan and his sons, who had saved Temuchin as a boy from the Tayichi'uts, were made lords of all the Kerait pastures.

As Temuchin ascended the throne of an emperor, his people gave him a new title. Since the Mongols believed that at the dawn of time the world had emerged in the centre of four oceans, they used the word 'ocean' to express the concept of a universe, and in recognition of Temuchin as ruler of the world and all men in it, they called him the Oceanic King – Genghis Khan.

Genghis Khan, ruler of the largest empire ever conquered by a single
commander, from the Imperial Chinese Portrait Gallery.

*(© Hulton Getty Picture Collection)*

After the fall of Bukhara, Genghis Khan addressed the citizens from the pulpit of a mosque and told them that he had come as the punishment of God for the wickedness of their rulers. Or 2780, f. 61r.

*(By permission of the British Library)*

The descendants of the hardy little horses which once carried Mongols into battle are still an essential element in the economy of the desolate steppes.
*(© Richard Harrington / RBO Camera Press)*

The felt tents, known as *gers*, in which modern Mongol nomads shelter from one of the most inhospitable climates on earth, have hardly changed since the days of Genghis Khan.
*(© György Lajos / Interfoto MTI, Hungary / Camera Press)*

Genghis Khan holds court flanked by the four sons to whom he bequeathed his empire. From the *Nusretname, a history of Cingiz Khan*. Or 3222, f. 43v.
(*By permission of the British Library*)

The mounted archers who made up the Mongol light cavalry provided Genghis Khan with the deadly combination of 'fire and movement' on which all his tactics were based. *(Courtesy of the Trustees of the V&A, V&A Picture Library)*

Heavy cavalry, the shock troops of the Mongol army, carrying twelve-foot lances and dressed in thick oxhide armour. From *The World History of Rashid-al-Din*. E.U.L. Or. Ms. 20, fol. 122 recto (A).
*(By permission of Edinburgh University Library)*

Like their medieval ancestors, modern Mongol herdsmen still cut out young horses for breaking with nooses on the end of long bamboo poles.

(*Herding Horses, Inner Mongolia. Artist: Vincent Haddelsey.* © *Private Collection / Bridgeman Art Library, London / New York*)

A Persian miniature depicting the Mongol invaders storming a citadel.
Ms. 7926 Sup. Persian 206. f. 149. (© *Bibliothèque Nationale, Paris, France/*
*Bridgeman Art Library, London/New York*)

Genghis Khan's great empire continued to grow after his death. Here, Mongols under the command of his grandson Hulegu are shown bombarding Baghdad with one of the lightweight siege-engines which they adopted during the invasion of China. Detail from: Ms. Sup. Pers. 1113 f. 180v–181.

# THE INVINCIBLE ARMY

The completion of one great task created others. The next was to make one nation out of a collection of tribes, not all of whom were even Mongol. At the Great Khuriltai and in the months that followed it, the new khan issued edicts providing for the pervasive government of all his subjects, and he did it in the way he knew best, as though they were an army.

Since the Mongols were illiterate and had no alphabet, the edicts were recorded by the former chief minister of the Naiman khan, a Uighur called Tata-tonga, whose highly cultured Turkish nation had ruled a steppe empire in the eighth century and now lived to the south beyond the Altai Mountains. Tata-tonga used the ancient Uighur script to record the edicts in Mongolian, and when he was not engaged in his new state duties, in accordance with the khan's orders, he gave reading and writing lessons to all the princes of the imperial blood.

Many of the edicts were designed to suppress the most common causes of feuding. Each clan was allocated its own inalienable grazing grounds. It was forbidden for any man to own a Mongol slave. The death penalty was made mandatory for traditional steppe crimes such as rustling and kidnapping. There were other edicts, however, which had a direct military purpose. A census was taken. With the exception of the shamans and the priests of other religions, all men between the ages of twenty and sixty were made liable for call-up to active service. Each one was assigned to a specific unit; and they were all required to take part in regular training. After a while, the nations that submitted voluntarily to Genghis Khan and a few of the most loyal tribes were allowed to form their own divisions, but in general, clansmen were dispersed among different units, so that their old allegiances could be replaced by loyalty to new comrades and obedience to new commanders.

The third great task, which could only be begun when the second had been completed, was the destruction of the Chin. For good reasons, the Chin were the enemies of unity on the steppes. Early in the recent tribal wars, Genghis Khan had realized that there could be no unity until their agents the Tatars had been destroyed. But he also understood human nature well enough to know that emperors as rich as the Chin would always be able to find replacements for the Tatars. If unity on the steppes was to survive, the Chin themselves would have to be destroyed, and for that the khan was going to need every trained man he could muster.

By the time he marched east towards the Great Wall, Genghis Khan's army was at least the equal of any other army in the world on the battlefield. Entirely composed of cavalry, it was an army for which the Mongols and their neighbours were ideal raw material. As hunters and herdsmen, they were trained from childhood in archery and horsemanship. They had incomparable powers of endurance. Unlike any other soldiers on earth, they lived on campaign in exactly the same way as they lived at home in peacetime. Their shelters were *gers*, the round felt tents which were also the homes of Mongol families, and in their camp, known as an *ordu*, which was the source of the English word 'horde', the way of life was very much the same for the army as it was for a clan.

Unlike a clan, the army was systematically organized and rigorously administered. Its units were formed in multiples of ten. At full strength a division, known as a *tumen*, contained 10,000 men. Each *tumen* was divided into ten regiments of a thousand called *minghans*, each of which contained ten squadrons of a hundred called *jaguns*, and these were divided into ten troops called *arbans*. The soldiers in the *arbans* elected their own commanders, who in turn elected the commanders of the *jaguns*, but the commanders of the *minghans* and *tumens* were appointed directly by the khan and given the military rank of *noyan*, which was the equivalent of a European baron. As evidence of their authority, the officers carried a gold or silver token, known as a *paize*, which varied in weight according to their rank and was inscribed with symbols that could be easily recognized by illiterate soldiers. The *noyan* who commanded a *tumen*, for example, carried a gold *paize* inscribed with a tiger's head.

The basic uniforms of all Mongols consisted of baggy trousers and long coats known as *kalats*, which were usually brown, grey or blue and were lined with fur in winter. Their long, laced-up leather boots were made without heels, and their conical caps had thick fur brims, which varied according to rank, from monkey for the commander of a *tumen* down through badger and fox to wolf for the commander of an *arban* and dog or goat for his troopers.

On the march, every man carried a large, waterproof, hide saddlebag, which could be inflated into a crude lifejacket for fording rivers, and in which he was required to carry a water-bottle, a cooking-pot, field rations and tools for repairing weapons and harness. In battle, he carried a sword, a wicker shield covered in leather, a lasso, a dagger strapped to the inside of his left forearm, two bows and two quivers containing arrows for every purpose from signalling to piercing armour. In addition, the light horseman carried three javelins and in some *tumens* wore a cuirass made of lacquered leather strips, and the heavy cavalryman, dressed in an iron helmet and an iron or oxhide cuirass, carried a battle-axe and a 12 ft lance with a hook below the point for dragging enemies from their saddles.

Whatever his role, however, the Mongol's most important weapon was his bow. Built on a wooden frame out of layers of bone and sinew, it had a pull of between 100 and 160 pounds and snapped out its arrows over an effective range of 360 yards. The Mongols could bend and string their bows in the saddle by placing one end between their feet and their stirrups, and they could shoot in any direction at full gallop, timing the release to come between the paces of their horses, so that the aim would not be deflected as the hooves hit the ground.

The horses themselves were as well trained as the men who rode them. Brave, hardy and slightly larger than the Mongolian horses of today, they were broken early, which made them docile, and then put out to grass for three years before being trained for battle. Their life could be harsh. On the march, each *tumen* was followed by its own herd of remounts, which enabled an army to move at speed for days on end, with each man changing mounts regularly and eating in the saddle or pausing briefly to slit the leg of a weak horse and drink its blood. Whenever possible the Mongols rode brood mares so that they could drink milk instead of blood. On a long march the weakest horses were often killed for food, and the mounts of messengers were sometimes ridden to death. But all this was done out of necessity not indifference. No armies, not even the armies of Islam, looked after their horses better than the Mongols. A horse that had been ridden in battle was a comrade in arms. When it was too old to fight it was put out to pasture and could never be eaten, although, if its master died, it might be killed and buried with him so that their spirits could ride together forever in the firmament. Horses played their part in folklore and ceremonies. White horses were regarded as sacred and fit only for shamans and the khan, and in the most splendid *tumen* in the Mongol army, the Imperial Guard, the men in each of the contingents, the Day Guard, the Night Guard, the Quiver Bearers and the Sword Bearers, were mounted on different-coloured horses.

The Imperial Guard, the *Kashik*, which always accompanied Genghis Khan, was the one unit in his army which was permanently on duty. Its ranks included his generals, the *orloks*, all his household, from councillors to servants, and

a son of every *tumen* commander, a privilege
which also prevented treachery by providing
him with hostages. But for the most part it
was composed of the most promising potential
commanders selected by competition from all
the *tumens* in the army. The *Kashik* was not only
the khan's ceremonial bodyguard, it was the
Mongol staff college. When they were not on
active service, the selected soldiers were waited
on by servants, so that they could devote all their
time to training, which included taking their turn
in attending the khan's councils and briefings.
No man could command a thousand men or
more until he had served in the *Kashik*, and in
an emergency every cadet in its ranks was
considered fit to command any other unit in the
Mongol army.

To provide all other Mongols with the
necessary military skills and knowledge, Genghis
Khan ordered that the traditional training in
archery and horsemanship should be made
compulsory for all male children, and that all
*tumens* should assemble regularly to practise their
simple battlefield manoeuvres. The most basic of
these was the battle formation, which consisted

of two lines of heavy cavalry with three lines of light cavalry behind them and three separate units of light cavalry far out to the front and on either flank. When the light cavalry to the front engaged the enemy with their bows, the light horsemen in the main body galloped forward through the heavy cavalry to join them. If an enemy attempted to attack a flank, the main body wheeled to face them, the light cavalry on that flank became the vanguard and the light cavalry which was now in the rear rode round to cover the unprotected flank.

Mongol light horsemen did not engage the enemy at close quarters. Instead, they galloped backwards and forwards in front of them, showering them with arrows. Once the enemy formations had been reduced to chaos by the casualties, the light cavalry broke away on either flank and the heavy cavalry charged through the centre to drive home the final blow. If the arrows from the front failed to break up the enemy formations, the light cavalry would attack a flank as well, and the heavy cavalry would ride round behind it to charge the enemy in the rear. Wherever possible, however, the Mongols' favourite tactic was to send forward a convincingly large unit which charged up to the enemy, broke and then fled as if in terror, drawing the enemy after it into a waiting arc of archers. In the ensuing carnage and confusion, the heavy cavalry, as always, completed the victory, advancing at the trot in silence, saving its hideous screams for the last moment when the huge kettle in the rear, the *naccara*, beat out the order to gallop.

These manoeuvres could be practised by comparatively small groups, but Genghis Khan also introduced an exercise which taught all his *tumens* to operate in unison on a large scale. Known as the great hunt and conducted as though it was a campaign, this expansion of the Mongols' favourite sport took place every spring in peacetime, lasted for three months and involved every available soldier. Flags were planted along a starting-line up to eight miles long to mark the assembly points for each *tumen*. Hundreds of miles ahead of them another flag was planted to mark the finishing point. At a signal from the khan, the entire army, dressed for battle, rode forward in a tight line driving the game ahead of it. As the weeks went by and the game built up, the wings of the army advanced further and further ahead of the centre, turning the line into a deep arc. Once the wings had passed the level of the finishing point, they turned inwards and eventually met far beyond it, enclosing the game in a circle. In the final phase the circle contracted until in the end the front ranks on either side of it could see each other clearly across a restless, disparate multitude of terrified animals.

On the morning of the last day the khan rode first into the ring to take his pick of the game. Until that moment, nobody had been allowed to kill; and where anyone had let even the smallest animal slip through the line, both he and his immediate commander had paid a forfeit. When the khan withdrew to the side to watch, his soldiers took their turns in groups, some demonstrating their marksmanship on the fastest and most distant deer, others recklessly displaying their courage by dismounting to challenge wild boar or even tigers to single combat. The first few hunts ended when the khan gave the order for the ring to divide, allowing the remaining animals to escape. After a while, however, it became the tradition for the hunt to end with a little ceremony, in which the old men and children who followed the hunt came to the khan and pleaded for the lives of the survivors.

Throughout the hunt the commanders signalled to each other constantly, altering their speed or indicating the positions and movements of herds. By day they used the flags that they employed on the battlefield, and by night, when the army halted and half the men held the line while the other half slept around their camp-fires, the flags were replaced by blazing torches. As on the battlefield, the more detailed messages were carried by dispatch riders. But for these horsemen, unlike the rest of the army, the duties of the great hunt were lighter than their other duties. Life in Genghis Khan's unique corps of couriers was much more demanding than it was in any other contemporary messenger service.

News had always travelled fast on the steppes. Every time a horseman brought a story to a camp, a fresh horseman set out to take it to the next camp as soon as he had heard it. As he did so often with many ideas, Genghis Khan took this simple custom and developed it into a complex communications system, the *ortoo*, which was capable of carrying messages from one side of his dominions to another at a rate of 120 miles a day.

Across the steppes he established a series of staging-posts which were only 25 miles apart, the distance that a good horse could cover at the gallop without pausing. As his armies advanced, new staging-posts were established in their wake, expanding his communications network with his empire. Each post, guarded by at least ten men, contained food, shelter and horses. The couriers, who bound their heads, chests and stomachs with tight bandages, also wore thick leather belts covered with bells, which alerted the posts to their approach and ensured that fresh horses were saddled and waiting on their arrival. At first, when the messages were long or vital, the entire journey might have to be covered by the same courier, but as time passed and more and more messages were written down the couriers began to change every day. On the road they were empowered to demand help from anyone they met. If a courier's mount tired, he could produce his *paize* and compel a traveller to exchange horses with him, although the traveller was then entitled to take his pick of the horses at the next post or else follow the courier and reclaim his own.

In every camp, and later in every town, there was an officer whose sole responsibility was to administer and protect the couriers' routes. His soldiers patrolled them and, after a while, as more and more literate nations became the subjects of the khan, his clerks recorded not only the times, names and destinations of every courier but also the details of every caravan and every foreigner that passed along them. Inevitably the guarded paths of the khan's couriers became commercial routes as well, and the staging-posts began to provide safe shelter for travellers. In the second half of the twelfth century, when the first European ambassadors, merchants and missionaries set out for the court of the great khan, they were astonished by the comfort of his staging-posts, and they reported with awe that unescorted travellers were safer in his empire than in any other kingdom on earth.

The essence of Genghis Khan's genius lay in his ability to recognize and develop a good idea, and above all in his instinctive capacity for

meticulous planning and detailed organization,
a capacity which was all the more extraordinary,
in a man who had received no education. His
tactics were the tactics which nomad archers had
been using for many hundreds of years. But after
constant practice Genghis Khan's Mongols were
able to employ them more effectively. Unlike
other medieval rulers, who appointed their
commanders on the basis of their birth, Genghis
Khan promoted men only on merit, and he trained
the men that he promoted. It was his confidence in
the ability of his officers and men, in the efficiency
of his support services and in the effectiveness
of his communications that enabled him to plan
and operate on a scale that had never before been
contemplated.

The tactics of the Mongol army would not have
been unfamiliar to the Scythian enemies of the
Roman Empire. With the exception of the bows,
its weapons and equipment were on the whole
no better than in other armies, and in some cases
they were worse. But its planning, training, officer
corps, command structure, logistics, intelligence
and communications were so far ahead of their
time that they would not have been unfamiliar to a

soldier of the twentieth century. At the beginning of the thirteenth century there was nothing else like it.

# The War with the Golden Emperors

The two years that followed the Great Khuriltai of 1206 were not entirely devoted to reorganization. Even in 1207 there were a few 'mopping up' operations in the west and an exploratory raid in the east. But Genghis Khan was now so famous and feared that his dominions began to expand without further need for fighting. At first it was only his most vulnerable and nervous neighbours in the western steppes who sent ambassadors to offer him tribute and allegiance, but in 1209 he received an ambassador from no less a prince than Barchuk, the 'Sacred King' of the Uighurs. Genghis Khan was so pleased with his new vassal that he gave him one of his daughters as a wife. The Uighurs provided him with a buffer state on his south-western flank, protecting his steppe empire from Kara-Khitai and the great Muslim empires beyond; and they provided his army with a splendid *tumen* of light cavalry dressed in yellow cloaks and black velvet caps. Above all, they provided him with his first literate subjects. At last he had the bureaucrats to administer his empire and manage the support services for his army.

During those first two years, however, Genghis Khan's empire was a great deal more secure than his throne. Many of his edicts had destroyed the traditional freedoms of the nomads. Many clansmen resented compulsory military service, many of their less competent hereditary leaders resented an army in which officers were promoted entirely on merit, and the discontented found themselves an unlikely figurehead in Kokochu, the son of Yesugei's old servant Monglik, whom the khan had made his chief shaman.

Genghis Khan respected Kokochu and he was grateful to him for providing celestial support. But the worldly and over-confident Kokochu, who gave himself the name Teb-tengri, 'Most Heavenly', was too ambitious to be content with the power of a shaman. He began by creating discord in the new royal family, turning the khan against his brother Kasar by warning him that, in a new vision, Mongke Tengri had revealed that Kasar might also rule the world. Although Kasar was one of his best generals, Genghis Khan had been wary of him for several years. At one time he had suspected that he was negotiating with Senggum and Wang Khan. On the basis of no more than the dream of a shaman, Genghis Khan deprived Kasar of his command and arrested him; and it was only the furious intervention of their mother that saved Kasar from imprisonment or worse.

While his trusting ruler continued to indulge him, even to the extent of allowing him to be impertinent in public, Kokochu set up his own camp and began to build his own army, attracting disaffected officers with promises of power and winning over superstitious soldiers with conjuring tricks and false prophecies. But his vanity got the better of him when the khan's youngest brother, Temuge, sent a messenger to demand the return of the hundreds of soldiers who had deserted from his *tumen*. The messenger was whipped and sent back on foot carrying his saddle. When Temuge, a prince of the imperial blood, came in person to make his demand, he was seized by Kokochu's seven brothers and forced to kneel in supplication before him.

Temuge rode to the imperial *ordu* and arrived very early in the morning at the khan's huge carpet-lined *ger*, which was mounted permanently on a wagon so heavy that it took twenty-two oxen to haul it. Exercising his privilege as an *orlok*, he strode unannounced into the khan's presence, knelt by his bed and indignantly reported his humiliation. Once again it was Genghis Khan's senior wife Borte who opened his eyes to the threat of a rival. Sitting up in the bed beside him and clutching the fur rug that covered them to her breasts, she warned him that there would be no dominions for her sons to inherit if the shaman's insolence went unpunished. Genghis Khan spoke quietly to his brother. 'When Kokochu comes here today,' he said, 'do as you like with him.'[1]

When Kokochu arrived that afternoon, Temuge challenged him and a traditional wrestling match was arranged. But as the haughty shaman was making his way through the camp to the place appointed for the contest, he was seized by three waiting wrestlers. On Temuge's instructions, they dragged him into the wagon park, broke his back and left him dying in the dust.

The brutal but easy murder of a man who claimed to have magical powers discredited him in the eyes of his gullible followers. Without him they were too ineffectual to be a threat. But there was still a potential threat to the khan's security among the rest of his soldiers. Mongol soldiers fought for plunder not pay. In the two years that followed the Great Khuriltai every able-bodied man in central Asia had been required to take part in regular training, but only a few of them had seen active service and even fewer had profited from it. In the long term a campaign against the Chin might be a strategic necessity, but in the short term it was a political expedient.

Before crossing the Gobi desert and marching deep into China, Genghis Khan had to secure his flanks. His left was already safe: the far eastern steppes were occupied by his friends the Ongguts, with whom he had strengthened his alliance by marrying one of his daughters to a son of their khan. But his right was dominated by the independent Tangut kingdom of Hsi-Hsia. The first step in a campaign against the Chin had to be an attack on Hsi-Hsia, not only because it would secure the flank but also because it would give the Mongols valuable experience in fighting against men who fought on foot as well as on horses and who lived in cities with walls around them.

The Mongols had made their first raid against the Tanguts in 1205 and had come back with huge herds, including thousands of camels. They made a second profitable raid in 1207, but this time they came back baffled by city walls. The Mongols were a match for any other army on the battlefield, but cavalry could not storm walls or conduct sieges. Although there was as yet very little experience to draw on, rudimentary siegecraft became one of the topics studied by the cadets in the Imperial Guard and every *tumen* in the army was equipped with storming ladders and sacks that could be turned into sandbags.

At the beginning of 1209 the Mongols returned to Hsi-Hsia, this time with Genghis Khan himself in command. In May they stormed and captured the city of Wolohai. In August they defeated a

Tangut army, capturing its general, and laid siege to the capital, Ning-Hsia, on the Yellow River. In October, when the rains raised the level of the river, the khan lost patience and dammed it, diverting its waters into the city. By the end of the year the Tangut king, Li Anquan, was contemplating surrender. But in January 1210, the dam broke and flooded the Mongol camp. With both parties now equally discomfited, the two rulers negotiated. The Tangut king swore allegiance to the Mongol Khan, gave him one of his daughters as a wife and paid his first tribute in wool, silk, falcons and rare white camels. But he refused to provide auxiliaries, pleading with some justification that his city-dwelling soldiers would be useless on a long march, and sneering rashly that his new sovereign did not deserve to be a great khan if he did not have enough soldiers of his own. For the time being the objective was to secure the right flank, and with the Tangut king's allegiance this had been achieved, but his refusal to provide soldiers was an insolence which Genghis Khan was never to forgive or forget.

In March 1211, after spending three days in solitary contemplation on the sacred mountain,

Genghis Khan marched east and began the war
that was to last beyond his lifetime. He was well
informed. He had received detailed reports from
Muslim merchants and discontented defectors.
The Chin emperor had half a million infantry
and 150,000 cavalry. They were ill prepared,
but even so, after leaving his brother Temuge to
maintain order in his vast steppe empire with a
mere two *tumens*, the most that Genghis Khan
could muster was seven *tumens*. Since they
cannot all have been at full strength, his total
striking force probably consisted of no more
than 65,000 horsemen.

The Mongol army crossed the Gobi Desert in
several columns and joined to enter China beyond
the crumbling northern tip of the Great Wall, at a
point where the Chin had built defences of their
own. As was their custom, the Chin employed a
nomad tribe to man these defences, and when
the Mongols approached, 10,000 horsemen were
waiting for them. But these horsemen had come
to join them not fight them. The men whom the
Chin employed to defend their frontier were
Ongguts. Without the loss of a single man, and
with his strength increased by the addition of a

precious *tumen*, Genghis Khan crossed the border into the Chin empire.

Defections were to be a problem for the Chin throughout the long war. Like any conquered people, the indigenous Han Chinese were happy to help an invader, at least until the invader's ferocity left them as terrified as their masters. The surviving settlers from the previous conquest, the Khitans, who made up a good proportion of the Chin cavalry and officer corps, were seldom more than unwilling mercenaries and were often ready to change allegiance, although usually only in the hope that the invader would restore them to their former power. Even some of the Chin commanders were so disillusioned by their decadent rulers that they were ready to assist in their downfall; and for the sake of their support in his most hazardous campaign, Genghis Khan seemed ready to modify his previously uncompromising attitude towards treachery. Out of the first four cities to be taken by the Mongols, one was surrendered without a fight by a Chin commander who was immediately put in charge of a *minghan*. Soon afterwards, when a senior Khitan officer was sent to negotiate a truce, he defected without even negotiating and took command of a newly formed *tumen* of Chinese rebels and experienced Mongols.

The fighting that followed struck terror throughout northern China. The Mongols divided their forces. Cities and towns that could be taken easily were sacked. Cities that were well defended were ignored. Mongol armies struck, vanished and reappeared soon afterwards, ravaging the countryside hundreds of miles away. The Chin were as baffled by the Mongols' mobility as the Mongols still were by their best city walls. Only twice did the Chin attempt a major engagement in the field, and both times it ended in disaster, once when they fell for a false retreat and once when their own retreating cavalry collided with their infantry, creating such chaos that the whole army fled. In the ensuing chase the Mongols followed them for 30 miles, shooting and hacking them down like game. After that, for the rest of the year, the Chin confined themselves to the limited risk of skirmishing and the comparative safety of the most baffling walls.

At the end of the summer the advancing Mongols reassembled on the plain outside Zhongdu and saw the magnificent Chin capital for the first time. The wall that surrounded it was 18 miles long, 40 feet tall, 50 feet wide at the base and crowned with no less than 900 towers. In front of the wall there were three deep moats, and far out in front of these, covering the four main roads to the city, there were four separate forts, from which the garrisons could launch attacks on the rear of any army that assaulted the city. Each fort was a mile square. It had its own supplies and armoury, and it was connected to the city by an underground tunnel.

An assault was out of the question, and so too was a siege. Within a month Genghis Khan's horses had eaten all the grass and left him with no choice other than to retire. As he was preparing to leave, however, The Chin emperor sent a Khitan general to negotiate a peace. Since the emperor was in an unassailable position, it was clear that the emissary had really been sent to find out what he could about the Mongol's strength, but, being a Khitan, he gave away more than he learned. He revealed that the emperor was threatened by court intrigue, that the Sung emperor in the south was watching and waiting

77

for a chance to intervene and, the most useful piece of information of all, that the Khitan exiles who lived beyond the Great Wall in the ancient homeland of the Chin were considering a rebellion against their Chin overlords. Genghis Khan took the hint. He refused to negotiate and set out at once north-eastwards towards the wall and the green pastures of Manchuria, where he rested his army for the winter, seized all the herds in the Chin emperor's stud farms and made a treaty with the Khitans.

In the following spring, with the support of an army commanded by Jebe, the Khitans of Manchuria rose in rebellion and laid siege to the old Chin capital at Liaoyang. When an assault failed, Jebe ordered everyone to abandon their camp. For two days they rode away. Then they turned and galloped back to find the gates open and the citizens looting their tents. The city was taken, the garrison was slaughtered and the Khitans transferred their allegiance from the Chin emperor to the Mongol khan.

Meanwhile Genghis Khan continued the devastation of the previous year, until a wound at the siege of Dadong forced him to withdraw and leave the campaign to his youngest son Tolui. Next year, 1213, he came back for the third time, and once more the Mongol armies converged on Zhongdu. Within the city their reappearance brought panic to the streets and deadly conspiracies to the palace. While three good generals defected, a cowardly and ambitious one, a eunuch called Hushahu, murdered the city governor and the emperor, seized the reins of government for himself and installed the crown prince as a puppet emperor. Soon afterwards, however, an apprehensive subordinate murdered Hushahu and presented his head to the terrified young emperor.

While the Chin court was diverted by intrigue, Genghis Khan left the still impregnable city and attacked a few dozen that were not. By the time his army returned for yet another winter in Manchuria they had captured ninety more towns and cities. Through experience and the advice of defectors, the steppe horsemen had become more than proficient at siegecraft. Each *tumen* was now accompanied by a full siege-train, partly manned by mercenary Chinese engineers. The largest ballistae and catapults were carried on wagons, but with the ingenuity of nomads the Mongols had devised ways of dismantling the lighter siege-engines and carrying them quickly into position on the backs of tough little ponies. In long sieges, as in other armies, the Mongols used prisoners to build the ramparts for their siege-engines, but unlike other armies they also saved casualties by forcing prisoners to go ahead of them when they were storming breaches.

By the end of April 1214, the khan's army was again assembled outside Zhongdu, only this time the four outlying forts had been captured. When the khan sent ambassadors offering terms, the Emperor Hsuan-tsung, who did not know that the Mongols were short of supplies, accepted readily. Recognizing the Mongol khan as his overlord, he gave him one of his sisters as a bride and presented him with 3,000 horses and 500 child slaves. At the end of May, laden with all the gold and silver they could carry, and followed by many thousands of prisoners, the Mongols turned back towards the steppes. Halting at the oasis of Dolon-nor, they separated all the craftsmen, scholars, physicians and artists from the train of prisoners and then slaughtered the useless remainder.

Genghis Khan was still at Dolon-nor, waiting for the cooler weather before he crossed the Gobi Desert, when he received the news that the terrified Chin emperor had abandoned Zhongdu and moved his capital south to Kaifeng. Furiously convinced that the treacherous young emperor had broken their treaty and was preparing to raise a new army, he ordered his own soldiers back to China.

Subodei led an army eastwards, fighting his way across Manchuria and eventually winning the submission of Korea. Mukali followed him, devastating southern Manchuria sufficiently to ensure the newly won independence of the Khitans and prevent the Chin emperor's kinsmen from coming to his assistance. Then he turned south, sacking everything in his path. By September his vanguard had reached Zhongdu. Within a month he had invested it so effectively that it was completely cut off. Every army that the emperor sent north to relieve it was intercepted and destroyed. Without supplies, the citizens of Zhongdu were soon reduced to cannibalism. In May 1215, when his officers refused to follow him in a last desperate sortie, the commander of the garrison committed suicide. Soon afterwards the exhausted and demoralized city was captured in an assault by no more than 5,000 men. The plundering that followed lasted for a month. Thousands were killed. When houses caught fire they were left to burn. A few years later, when the city was visited by ambassadors from the Sultan of Khwarazm, they found the streets still slippery with human fat, and when they asked what the white hill was outside the walls, they were told that it was a pile of human bones.

After appointing Mukali viceroy with new instructions to conquer all the Chin dominions, Genghis Khan returned to the steppes. He had gained a lot from his campaign besides vassals and riches. The last caravan of plunder from Zhongdu had been accompanied by Yeh-lu Ch'u-ts'ai, the Chin emperor's brilliant young Khitan chancellor, who was soon to be the Khan's chancellor. The Mongol army had acquired a medical corps, manned by Chinese physicians. From now on there would be a dressing-station in every camp. Above all, from a military point of view, the army was no longer daunted by walls. It had acquired a formidable siege-train, and it had acquired it just in time. Within four years Genghis Khan was at war with the most powerful ruler in Asia, marching west on the astounding campaign which, more than any other, was to contribute to his twin reputations as a monster and a military genius.

# THE ROAD TO SAMARKAND

When the founders of the Chin empire invaded northern China, the previous conquerors, the Khitans, were scattered across Asia. Those that had fled north to Manchuria or remained to become subjects of the Chin were now fighting against them alongside the Mongols. But while these Khitans were exacting retribution in China, the more successful Khitan exiles, the founders of Kara-Khitai in the west, were being overwhelmed and dispossessed of yet another empire.

Soon after he returned to the steppes, Genghis Khan learned of their misfortune, and he learned also that the cause of it was his only surviving enemy from the wars on the steppes, Kuchlug, the Naiman prince who had persuaded his father to attack the Mongols. The opportunist Kuchlug had married the daughter of the ruler of Kara-Khitai, the Gurkhan, and to please her had converted from Christianity to Buddhism. When the neighbouring Sultan Muhammad of Khwarazm expanded his empire so much that he no longer felt obliged to pay tribute to Kara-Khitai, Kuchlug had entered into secret negotiations with him. The sultan had destroyed the Khitan army, and Kuchlug had imprisoned the Gurkhan and replaced him on the throne. Since then, like most opportunists, he had given way to his greed and imposed crippling taxes on his subjects, and like many converts he had become intolerant. He forbade all public services, and when the Imam of Khotan refused to convert to Buddhism, he crucified him on the gates of his college.

Genghis Khan had two good reasons for interfering. In the first place, Kuchlug was assembling a Naiman army, which threatened his south-western flank. Second, quite apart from any strategic or political considerations, he had learned that Kuchlug had killed Arslan, the khan of the Karluk. Arslan had voluntarily sworn allegiance to Genghis Khan shortly after the sacred king of the Uighurs and he had been married to one of his granddaughters. As Arslan's Mongol overlord,

Genghis Khan was obliged to avenge him. In 1218 Jebe was sent into Kara-Khitai with two *tumens*. For men who had recently fought in China, it was not a difficult campaign. When he reached the gates of the capital, Kashgar, Jebe simply announced that within the Mongol empire all religions were respected equally. The Muslims, who were by far the majority of the population, rose in rebellion and opened the gates, and when Kuchlug tried to escape, they caught him and killed him.

Like Kuchlug, his ally Sultan Muhammad was an opportunist. His empire had been founded by a Turkish mercenary called Khutbeddin Muhammad. Although most of his indigenous subjects were Persian, the majority of the soldiers in his huge army were descendants of Khutbeddin's mercenaries. When he inherited Khwarazm in 1200 Muhammad used his army to conquer his western neighbour, the Persian kingdom of Khurasan, and when the Mongols invaded Kara-Khitai, he marched almost unopposed in to his eastern neighbour, the empire of Transoxiana, which lay between Kara-Khitai and the Aral Sea. Without really testing his army against a worthy adversary, Sultan Muhammad had made himself the most powerful and richest ruler in Asia. His empire now stretched westward from the River Indus and the Hindu Kush to the Persian Gulf and the Caspian Sea, and the richest of his jewels was his latest acquisition. With its south-western and north-eastern borders formed by the Amu Darya and Syr Darya, rivers which were known in the west as the Oxus and the Jaxartes, Transoxiana straddled the trade routes to the east. At the eastern end of the road, beside the Syr Darya, stood the city of Khojend; at the western end, near the Amu Darya, stood Bukhara, famous for its carpets and universities; and in the centre stood the sultan's new capital, the beautiful city of gardens, canals and palaces, Samarkand.

In 1218 Muhammad concluded a commercial treaty with Genghis Khan, who controlled the trade routes beyond Transoxiana. Soon afterwards the first caravan of Muslim merchants from Mongolia, accompanied by a Mongol ambassador, arrived at the city of Otrar, which stood on the Syr Darya to the north of Khojend. When the governor of the city reported to the sultan that the merchants might be spies, the sultan replied that if the case could be proved they were all to be put to death. They may well have been spies. Most merchants were spies in those days. Nevertheless, there was obviously nothing to be learned about the border city that the Mongols did not know already. The suspicion did not warrant the affront of an investigation. But 500 camels laden with gold, silk and sable were too much of a temptation for the governor. Without so much as questioning them, he murdered the ambassador, the merchants and even their camel drivers and confiscated their property. When Genghis Khan sent another ambassador asking reasonably that the governor should be brought to trial, the vain, proud and recklessly overconfident sultan burned the beards and hair of his two escorts and gave them his head to carry back to the khan. The next and last message was the brief, inevitable declaration of war.

In preparation for the Mongol advance, the sultan drew up an astonishing army of 500,000 Turks and Persian auxiliaries in a 500-mile cordon along the southern bank of the Syr Darya. Their camps were luxurious, their burnished armour glittered, their horses were thoroughbred Arabs and the swords of their officers were bejewelled.

But they were ill-trained and inexperienced. The Persians were not entirely averse to the idea of an invasion. Even some of the Turkish officers had lost confidence in the sultan. His able and courageous son Jalal ad-Din, who was the antithesis of his father, argued that their best chance of victory lay in advancing into the steppes at once and attacking before the Mongol forces had time to concentrate. But his father, confident in what he knew was bound to be a huge numerical superiority, preferred to do nothing and wait for the arrival of the impudent nomad.

Across the steppes Genghis Khan's messengers rode from camp to camp summoning the *tumens* to assemble. Meanwhile, in the Uighur territory, north-east of Kara-Khitai, the khan and Subodei met to plan the campaign. Jalal ad-Din was right: while they were assembling, the Mongols were vulnerable. But since Jebe was still in Kashgar with two *tumens*, the khan sent his eldest son Jochi to join him with orders to attack the Khwarazmian right flank and keep the sultan busy until the rest of the army was ready.

Jochi and Jebe crossed the Tien Shan mountains in thick snow and advanced along the Ferghana

Valley. When news of an approaching army reached the Khwarazmian lines, Jalal ad-Din rode down to meet them with 50,000 men. The Mongols made a feigned retreat and then turned to attack in the foothills of the mountains, but they were too few and too exhausted to do more than hold their own. Eventually they broke off and fell back. The inconclusive and costly engagement, which the Khwarazmians saw as a victory, helped to raise morale along the Syr Darya. But to the Mongols, who could not yet have known that the enemy commander was too incompetent to exploit an advantage, it had achieved its objective. The sultan had been distracted and Genghis Khan was now ready to take the offensive.

The Mongol army, 200,000 strong, the largest ever assembled by Genghis Khan, advanced in four groups. The first, led by Genghis Khan and Subodei, and the second, led by two of the khan's sons, Ogodei and Chaghatai, set out from the Irtysch river towards the north of the sultan's line. The third and fourth, led by Jebe and Jochi, advanced towards the south of the line from Kashgar. When the two northern armies reached Otrar, in the autumn of 1219, Ogodei and Chaghatai laid siege to the city while Genghis Khan and Subodei turned north and vanished.

The garrison of Otrar held the walls for five months. When these fell, they held the citadel for another two months while the Mongols slaughtered the helpless citizens. In the final assault, the desperate governor, who knew that he could expect no mercy, climbed on to the roof of his house with his wife and flung tiles at the attackers. Since they had been ordered to take him alive, the Mongols dug under the building to make it collapse, hauled him from the rubble and led him away for execution.

In the south, Jochi advanced to make hit-and-run attacks on the Khwarazmian line and keep as much of it occupied as he could, while Jebe turned away and worked his way round the right flank. After a few successful attacks, Jochi divided his strength, sending the bulk to attack Khojend and leading the remainder northwards. Khojend fell easily, but as the Mongols stormed through the gates, the ingenious governor, Timur Malik, used barges to transport the surviving citizens on to a fortified island in the middle of the river and continued to hold it with only a thousand men.

When the Mongols attempted to attack in barges, his archers drove them off. When they began to build a stone causeway, his archers used their own barges to attack the builders. When inevitably, despite the casualties, the causeway had almost reached the island, he crowded his survivors into his barges, broke through the chain which had been stretched from bank to bank and escaped northwards with the flow of the river.

As he was returning southwards along the east bank of the river, Jochi was met by a messenger who told him what was happening. Jochi halted, built a barricade of boats from the nearest village and manned it with archers and even artillery. He had only just completed his work when the convoy of barges appeared with Mongol horsemen trotting helplessly along the banks beside it. But Timur Malik had put horses in the barges. When he saw the barricade he turned on to the west bank, landed as many men as he could and with fresh horses outran his pursuers. At last the Mongols had met a worthy adversary in Khwarazm, and they saluted him as such. According to the unlikely sagas which recorded his exploit throughout both the steppes and the world of Islam, he was the only survivor of Khojend to escape.

When he heard that Khojend had fallen and that Jebe was advancing into Transoxiana from the south, the sultan moved from Bukhara to Samarkand and sent his last 50,000 reserves to meet Jebe. When the news came that the reserves had been cut to pieces, even Sultan Muhammad realized that his position was precarious. His line on the Syr Darya was pinned down by Jochi, Jebe was advancing behind it, and he could not send more men to meet Jebe without weakening the garrison of his capital. Then, as if all this was not enough, news came that yet another army had appeared mysteriously 400 miles behind his lines.

Genghis Khan and Subodei were outside the gates of Bukhara. They had crossed the desert of Kizil-kum, which the sultan's Khwarazmians believed to be impenetrable. Well informed by his advance intelligence, Genghis Khan had turned north from Otrar to find one of the Turkoman guides who knew and understood the shifting red sands, and with one of these at the head of his army he had advanced unseen beyond Bukhara along a route that was known ever afterwards as 'the Khan's Road'.

In surrounding Bukhara, Genghis Khan and Subodei left one of the gates unguarded, hoping that the garrison might be tempted to come out and fight in the open. But the 20,000 mercenary horsemen who came out were only pretending to attack. As soon as they were clear of the city and their employers, they fled. The Mongols let them go and then, next day, when their path was blocked by the river, came up behind them and annihilated them.

While the governor and his garrison withdrew to the citadel, the Persian inhabitants sent their imams to surrender the city to Genghis Khan. In so doing they saved their lives. Although they were all driven in terror out of the city, they were allowed to return to their houses as soon as the khan's soldiers had finished pillaging them. But the city did not survive its capture. In the assault on the citadel, the doomed garrison shot burning tar from its ballistae, some of which set fire to the wooden houses. By the time the citadel had been taken and the Mongols and citizens were able to turn their attention to the flames, Bukhara was blazing beyond salvation. Before leaving, Genghis Khan assembled the citizens and addressed them from an open-air pulpit, declaring that their misfortunes had been brought upon them by the sins of their rulers and that he and his soldiers were the punishment of God.

In the weeks that followed, the plan of campaign reached its climax. Everything so far had been co-ordinated. While Jochi held the attention of the line on the Syr Darya, Jebe and Genghis Khan had been able to work their way round each flank. Now, from the four points of the compass, the Mongols converged on Samarkand. Ogodei and Chaghatai marched west from Otrar and then came down from the north. Jochi advanced from Khojend in the east. Jebe came up from the south. Genghis Khan and Subodei came from the west.

The great city that had been expected to hold out for at least a year was taken after only ten days, on 19 March 1220. As at Bukhara, half the garrison came out to meet its end beyond the walls, the citizens opened the gates and, with the exception of the 300 expert craftsmen who were impressed into Mongol service, were allowed to buy their freedom for 200,000 dinars each. When the remainder of the garrison surrendered the citadel a few days later, they were all massacred.

The fall of Samarkand did not bring the expected end to the war. The sultan had escaped before the Mongols arrived, and the best of his soldiers were now leaving him and rallying to his son. Nevertheless, despite Subodei's protests that the primary objective had to be the destruction of Jalal ad-Din, Genghis Khan still believed that the war could be ended with the capture or death of the sultan, and he ordered Jebe and Subodei to take two *tumens* and hunt him down.

By the time they reached Nishapur, where the sultan had last been seen, he had fled north to Kazvin. He was now so afraid of his own army that he was escorted only by his bodyguards, and even among them he was so careful that he slept secretly in a different tent each night. His fear was justified. One morning he woke in a simple soldier's tent to find that the splendid but empty royal tent had been shot through with arrows. From town to town Jebe and Subodei followed him, until at last, by less than a bowshot, he escaped from them in a boat to the island of Abescum on the Caspian Sea. There, on 10 January 1221, he died of pleurisy, in such poverty that there was nothing to bury him in but a torn shirt.

When he heard of the sultan's death, Genghis Khan summoned Subodei to a conference in Samarkand. At last the master strategist persuaded him that Jalal ad-Din had to be defeated and defeated quickly. If all the soldiers in Khwarazm rallied to him, he could still recover his empire. But Subodei also asked to be excused from the campaign and requested instead that he and Jebe should be allowed to take their two *tumens* north of the Caspian and reconnoitre the western steppes. The khan agreed. While Subodei returned to join Jebe by the Caspian, the great conqueror marched south on the dreadful campaign that was to leave the bloodiest stain on his grim reputation.

What followed was not to be equalled until the twentieth century. The Mongol army spread out and marched through Khurasan, razing cities and slaughtering everyone within their walls. Since most of the inhabitants of the countryside had taken refuge in the cities, the numbers of dead were even greater than their populations. The lowest contemporary estimates were 700,000 each for Merv and Balkh and a million and a half each for Herat and Nishapur, where the heads of men, women and children were collected in separate piles and even the dogs and cats were slaughtered.

The terror may have deterred the Persian population from supporting their prince, but his Turkish soldiers fought on and even at one point held off a Mongol attack. Eventually, however, Jalal ad-Din was cornered on the banks of the River Indus. When his position became hopeless, he urged his horse into the river, swam across with his standard in his hand and escaped across a thousand miles to the shores of the Caspian, where, like many other fugitives from the Mongols, he lived as a bandit until murdered by a Kurd.

The war was over. In the east Mukali was still fighting the resilient Chin. But in the west Genghis Khan was master of all the lands now known as Iran, Afghanistan, Pakistan, Turkmenistan and Uzbekistan. As he rode back from the last battle, he greeted the Persian people as his subjects. As his Khitan chancellor had told him, the time had come to make an end of killing.

Genghis Khan spent the summer of 1222 in the pastures below the Hindu Kush, a landscape which he preferred to the irrigated farmlands of Khwarazm. Here he entertained the great Taoist philosopher Changchun, who had travelled 2,000 miles to be with him. The khan had an awed respect for the sage, although his main preoccupation seems to have been to discover whether or not the old man had the secret of eternal life. When the two withdrew to Samarkand for the winter, he showed no similar respect for the imams of Islam or their great civilization. He had conquered, and even destroyed, some of the most beautiful cities in the world. But to Genghis Khan the greatest treasures of his new dominions were the wines of Shiraz and Arab horses. As soon as he had appointed military governors, he returned to the steppes. At heart, 'the Emperor of Mankind' was a nomad.

# SEVEN

# THE LAST CAMPAIGN

In the spring of 1223 Genghis Khan left Samarkand and moved back to the steppes, to the game-filled valley of the River Irtysh, where he spent almost two years hunting and resting. It was his first long rest for many years, and it was to be his last. Only two things spoiled it. One was the news brought home by Subodei that Jebe, 'the Arrow', had died of a fever on the way back from Russia. The other was a quarrel with his eldest son Jochi.

Some said that Jochi was sulking because his father had not named him as his heir. Before setting out to attack Khwarazm, the khan had called his sons together, and when it looked as though he was about to name Jochi, Chaghatai had protested, calling his brother a 'Merkit bastard'.[1] Eventually the khan had appointed a compromise candidate, the affable and intemperate Ogodei, to succeed him as supreme khan, and beneath Ogodei's authority he had assigned individual dominions to each of his other sons.

But if Jochi resented this, he showed no sign of it. He took on the most difficult responsibility in the campaign that followed and he carried it out effectively and enthusiastically. The only sign of discord came later. To his credit, Jochi vehemently denounced the wanton slaughter in Khurasan. After that, as he often did, he kept himself to himself. When his father summoned him to his camp on the Irtysh, he did not go, claiming that he was ill. But it later became known that he had not been ill, he had been hunting; and when the khan ordered him to take a *tumen* west, meet Jebe and Subodei and assist them in the conquest of the Bulgars on the upper Volga, he turned up late. Subodei had only come back because the khan had sent a messenger ordering him to bring Jochi home. Perhaps at Subodei's prompting, Jochi entered the huge pavilion where his father was holding an audience, took his hand and, kneeling in front of him, placed it on his forehead in the traditional gesture of submission. Only after the submission had been accepted did he present his father with the gift he had brought, a herd of several thousand horses. Jochi's disobedience was never spoken of again, but when he died not long afterwards, the court gossips speculated that the khan had arranged to have him poisoned.

After the audience, Subodei reported on his reconnaissance to his khan. It was a detailed and down-to-earth report, but behind it lay an astonishing adventure. The ride of Jebe and Subodei, which was to become legendary throughout Asia, was probably the greatest achievement of cavalry in the entire history of war. In two years, with 20,000 men, they had ridden over 5,500 miles, fought more than a dozen battles against superior numbers and come home with a profusion of plunder and priceless information. The steppes stretched across Russia to the borders of Hungary and beyond. The people who lived there were mostly Turko-Mongol nomads. They were ideal dominions and subjects for a Mongol emperor, and it was Subodei's dream to conquer them all. It was a dream that he was one day to fulfil, but for the time being the khan had other duties for him in the east.

By contrast, the people of Europe knew a great deal less about the Mongols than Subodei had learned about them. The Russians persuaded themselves that the raiders would not return, and in the rest of Europe the scraps of information that came out of the Middle East were either modified to fit in with legends or else manipulated for propaganda.

While Genghis Khan was preparing to invade Khwarazm, Pope Honorius III was trying unsuccessfully to persuade the kings of Europe to mount another crusade. In an attempt to help him, the Bishop of Acre, in Syria, wrote a report in which he claimed that the great Christian king of the Orient, Prester John, was assembling an army to march against the Saracens. Soon afterwards, remembering that the legend of Prester John was almost a hundred years old, some of his clergy wrote additional reports in which the eastern king was identified as Prester John's grandson, King David of India. At last the Christian kings of Europe began to rally their armies, eager to share in what promised to be the final glory.

In 1221, after the crusade had ended in disaster, the Syrian clergy learned to their astonishment that there really was an army advancing from the east and that it had taken Samarkand. What they were never to know was that there was even more truth to their story than that. There were Nestorian Christians in the army, Keraits and Naimans, and their commander was the adopted son, not the grandson, of an oriental Christian king.

By the end of 1225 'King David of India' was riding east again. His Tangut vassals in Hsi-Hsia had rebelled. The time had come to wreak retribution on them for refusing to provide soldiers for the campaigns in both China and Khwarazm.

The invasion began towards the end of 1226 and soon afterwards Genghis Khan became ill. Nobody knows for certain what was wrong, some chroniclers said malaria, others that a fall from his horse had caused internal injuries. His officers pleaded with him to return to the steppes, but he insisted on remaining with his army. While the khan grew weaker and weaker, his soldiers ravaged Hsi-Hsia. As they had done before, they built dams and diverted rivers into cities. In one spectacular victory, when the Tangut cavalry attempted to charge across the frozen floodwaters of the Yellow River, the Mongols wrapped the hooves of their horses in felt and charged sure-footedly into their flank, cutting them to pieces as they slid out of control and crashed into each other.

By the beginning of August 1227, the Mongols were besieging the capital, Ning-Hsia. When ambassadors came out to report that the Tangut king had died and that his son was ready to sue for peace, they were received by Mongol generals. Behind them, in the huge tent on a wagon, with Ogodei and Tolui beside him, Genghis Khan was also dying. His death, a few days later, in his sixtieth year, was kept secret, even from his soldiers. In accordance with his last wishes, the new Tangut king and his courtiers were executed when they came out to negotiate. Only after that were his soldiers told that he was dead, and in the storming of Ning-Hsia next day every citizen and animal within the walls was slaughtered.

Genghis Khan's coffin was carried back to northern Mongolia and buried in an unmarked grave on the side of Burkhan Kaldun. Two years later, forty fine horses and forty bejewelled, moon-faced virgins were sacrificed on the site to keep him company. Within a few more years the undergrowth had covered the grave so completely that it was lost. But a thousand miles across

the Gobi Desert from Ning-Hsia to northern
Mongolia is a long way for an unembalmed body
to travel in August and September. It may well be
that the coffin was empty long before it reached
the sacred mountain.

Unlike other great conquerors, Genghis Khan
has no tomb. But Genghis Khan left an empire
that kept growing after his death and founded
dynasties that ruled different parts of it for
centuries, an achievement which no other
conqueror has equalled. In the West, the
descendants of Jochi, khans of the Golden Horde,
ruled southern Russia for a hundred years. In
Iran, Tolui's son Hulegu was the first of the seven
Il-khans who ruled for almost as long. In India, in
the sixteenth century, a descendant of Chaghatai,
Babur, founded the great Moghul dynasty. In the
east, another of Tolui's sons, Khubilai, reunited
China and founded the Yuan dynasty.

As a soldier, Genghis Khan created an army
whose strategies and tactics have been an example
ever since. They were studied by Napoleon and
were still being taught to Russian cavalry officers
at the beginning of the twentieth century. Even
as recently as the Second World War, two of the

leading tank commanders, Rommel and Patton, were acknowledged students and admirers of the Mongol army.

On the basis of his achievements alone, Genghis Khan ranks high among the very greatest conquerors of history. If it were not for the horrifying bloodshed that accompanied those achievements, he might stand high above all of them.

# *NOTES*

### A Note on Transliteration

1   David Morgan, *The Mongols*, Oxford, Blackwell, 1986, Intro, p. 4.

### Chapter Two

1   *The Secret History of the Mongols*, paragraph 96, edited with French translation by P. Pelliot, Paris, Libraire d'Amerique et d'Orient, 1949. (English translation by James Chambers)

### Chapter Five

1   *The Secret History of the Mongols*, quoted in R. Grousset, *Conqueror of the World*, Edinburgh and London, Oliver & Boyd, 1967, p. 180.

### Chapter Seven

1   *The Secret History of the Mongols*, paragraph 254, quoted in P. Ratchnevsky, *Genghis Khan*, English translation, Oxford, Blackwell, 1991, p. 126.

# *B I B L I O G R A P H Y*

Boyle, J.A., transl., Ata Malik Juvayni, *The History of the World Conqueror*, Manchester, Manchester University Press, 1958 (reprinted 1997)

Chambers, James, *The Devil's Horsemen*, London, Weidenfeld & Nicolson, 1979

Grousset, René, *Conqueror of the World*, transl. D. Sinor and M. McKellar, Edinburgh and London, Oliver & Boyd, 1967

Cleaves, F.W., transl. *The Secret History of the Mongols*, Cambridge, Mass., Harvard University Press, 1982

Liddell Hart, B.H., *Great Captains Unveiled*, London, Blackwood, 1927

Martin, H.D., *The Rise of Chingis Khan and his Conquest of North China*, Baltimore, John Hopkins Press, 1950

Morgan, David, *The Mongols*, Oxford, Blackwell, 1986

Phillips, E.D., *The Mongols*, London, Thames & Hudson, 1969

Ratchnevsky, Paul, *Genghis Khan*, Oxford, Blackwell, 1991

Saunders, J.J., *The History of the Mongol Conquests*, London, Routledge & Kegan Paul, 1971